KNICKERS!

*6 sewing patterns for handmade lingerie including
French knickers, cotton briefs and saucy Brazilians*

DELIA ADEY & ERIKA PETO

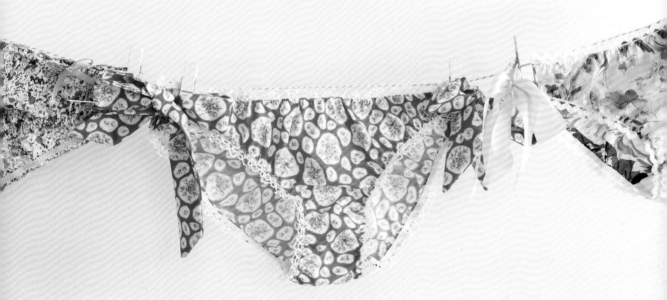

David and Charles

www.sewandso.co.uk

Contents

Introduction

Knickers, pants, panties, bloomers, briefs, shorties, drawers, pantaloons, tangas, thongs – they've had different names and shapes throughout history, changing with the shape and style of the fashion worn and the fabrics available. Our little book picks out our favourite shapes and fun styles that can be made at home with little expense.

Lingerie making has always had a little mystery about it but the truth is they're just smalls... and they make lovely little sewing projects. We hope to demystify this and make sewing your smalls fun.

If you're reading this in America (or anywhere else where pants mean trousers and knickers could mean anything at all), you might need to know that 'knickers' is a classic British term for ladies' underwear and carries with it the concept of frills, frivolity and fun. It's also something the Brits have been known to utter as an exclamation when things haven't gone quite as planned!

We hope you enjoy making these knickers, and then wearing your end products even more!

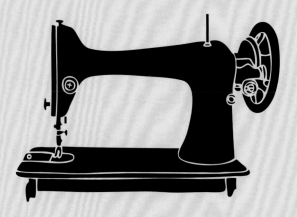

BEFORE YOU Begin

Materials

YOU HAVE A CHOICE TO MAKE BEFORE YOU SET OUT ON YOUR UNDERWEAR ODYSSEY:

WHAT FABRIC ARE YOU GOING TO MAKE YOUR KNICKERS FROM?

The knickers in this book use different fabrics and the pattern you are following will guide you. We have also given alternatives that can be used. So that you can make an informed decision, here is our overview of suitable materials and the qualities that each one has.

Woven cotton

Cotton is a natural woven fabric, which means that its fibres form a warp and a weft. The warp is the vertical fibre and the weft runs horizontally from one side to the other. The edge where the weft fibre curves round creates the selvedge, the non-fraying edge of the fabric. Cotton does not stretch when pulled horizontally or vertically. It does give a little when pulled diagonally. This is called the bias.

Cotton lawn

Cotton lawn is a plain weave textile, designed using high count yarns, which result in a silky smooth feel. It is beautiful and light and perfect for making underwear, and gives a silk-like feel while at the same time being easier to manage than silk when sewing.

Silk

Silk is the name of the fibre spun from insect larvae. The best known silk is from the larvae of the Mulberry silk worm, *Bombyx Mori*, which is reared in captivity for industry. They are larvae moths. Silk originates from Asia where it is still made today. It has always been associated with luxury products and favoured throughout history by royalty and the rich. It's a beautiful textile to wear, breathable, light and soft against the skin.

To sew with it is a bit tricky as it tends to slip and move when cutting. As you get more confident with sewing it is worth persevering with silk because of the lovely results that you can achieve.

Stretch cotton jersey

Jersey is a knit fabric originally made from wool but now made from a combination of wool, cotton and synthetic fibres. It was first made in Jersey (Channel Islands) in medieval times. As the fibres are knitted together instead of woven, a stretchy fabric is created. It is often used to make t-shirts and has become a staple of modern wardrobes.

By adding Lycra the jersey fabric has become even stretchier. Knickers are best made with a four-way stretch, a jersey with added Lycra. You can tell this by pulling it with your hands and feeling the amount of 'ping' it has when it returns to the pre-pulled shape. The more stretch in the fabric the more hold your underwear will have to stay up! It makes very comfortable underwear and is a modern favourite.

Stretch it and see!

A LITTLE LYCRA GOES A LONG WAY. TO FIND OUT IF A FABRIC MIGHT CONTAIN SOME, TRY THE FOLLOWING STRETCH TESTS.

ONE WAY STRETCH
Stretch on the cross grain and no recovery (no Lycra)

TWO WAY STRETCH
Stretch and recovery on the cross grain (contains Lycra)

FOUR WAY STRETCH
Stretch and recovery on the cross grain and the lengthwise grains (contains Lycra)

Lycra is a synthetic fibre which can be mixed with many other fabrics natural and synthetic; wool, cotton, nylon, polyester. It revolutionized clothing and underwear especially sports clothing. It is ideal for tight fitting garments and perfect for comfortable knickers.

Trims and Elastics

All knickers need some sort of trim or elastic to hold them up and to keep the garment in the required place against the body.

Knickers made from non stretch (woven) fabrics like cotton need to have elastic in the waistband and with most knickers, except for camisole knickers, around the legs. For the cotton original, and ribbon-tie knickers in this book we have used a knicker elastic approximately 1cm (½in) wide. Half of the elastic is made up of a frill or a loop, which sits over the edge of the knickers, to serve as a decorative edge. We've used the same size elastic on the waistband and the legs, but for different looks and designs vary the size of the two elastics.

When making knickers from stretch fabrics knicker elastic can be used but you could choose stretch lace which adds a more decorative finish. Stretch lace doesn't have the same elasticity as elastic but because the fabric is clinging to the body shape already the trim doesn't have to work as hard as the elastic on the cotton knickers. The result is a more comfortable feeling when worn. Stretch lace comes in various sizes from 1cm (½in) width up to 20cm (8in) wide. We use a 4cm (1½in) width for our knickers. Again, it overlaps the edge of the material and becomes a decorative feature to the garment. Stretch lace can also come with a variety of shaped edges, some are curved or scalloped which adds further to the design.

Finding the right trims can be fun and sometimes a seemingly never-ending mission! We always have our eyes peeled for new and old lace trims, and we stock a good selection at the Flo-Jo shop. We're forever on the look out for unusual and old pieces at antique fairs and markets. Unlike lace, elastic does have a shelf life and unfortunately does perish with age so be careful and test the stretch of your elastic if you are buying genuine vintage trims in this way.

Tools

KNICKER-MAKING TOOLS ARE NOT RARE OR UNUSUAL, IN FACT IF YOU DO A BIT OF SEWING ALREADY YOU WILL PROBABLY HAVE EVERYTHING YOU NEED.

The six projects in this book do all require a sewing machine, but you don't have to have an expensive or specialized one. The only requirement apart from a straight stitch is that it has a zig-zag stitch, which is a key part of applying elastic and so a key part in keeping your knickers up! Most modern machines, post 1950, have a zig-zag stitch, hand-powered machines tend not to.

Along with your fabric, elastic, lace and trimmings you with need a sharp pair of dressmaking scissors, threads and pins. Pinking shears are useful to prevent fabrics from fraying after you have cut out pattern pieces. But you won't need a giant sewing room – knickers are a nice size to work with so you don't even need much space.

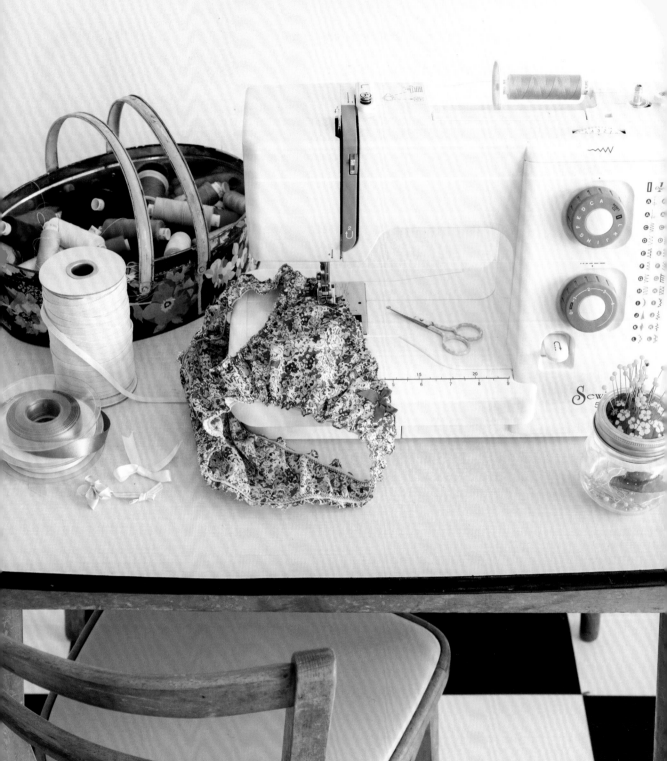

Making

The

KNICKERS

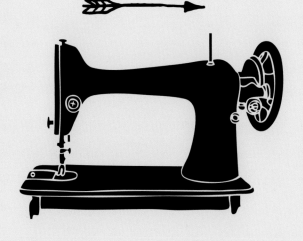

COTTON ORIGINAL

THIS KNICKER PATTERN MAKES A
MODERN CLASSIC SHAPE, WHICH SITS ON THE HIPS AND
COVERS THE BOTTOM. QUICK AND INEXPENSIVE, YOU MAY FIND
THAT IF YOU MAKE YOUR OWN CLOTHES THERE ARE OFTEN ENOUGH
LEFTOVER SCRAPS TO MAKE A MATCHING PAIR OF KNICKERS. PERFECT
FOR WEARING WITH SUMMER DRESSES – YOU WON'T MIND GETTING
CAUGHT IN A GUST OF WIND!

WE CUT THESE KNICKERS ON THE BIAS, WHICH ALLOWS A LITTLE MORE
EASE AND COMFORT TO WEAR. WORKING WITH LIGHTWEIGHT COTTON IS A
PERFECT START FOR NEWBIE KNICKER-MAKERS AS IT'S EASY TO HANDLE.
FRILLED KNICKER ELASTIC IS ADDED TO COVER THE RAW EDGES AND
CHANGING THE COLOUR AND TYPE OF FRILL CAN CHANGE THE LOOK.

You Will Need

50 x 55cm (20 x 22in) cotton fabric, poplin or lawn

15 x 10cm (6 x 4in) cotton jersey for gusset

2m (2 ¼yd) elastic, 1–1.5cm (½–⅝in) wide with a
frilled or crocheted edge

50cm (20in) satin ribbon, 9mm (½in) wide, to
decorate

Thread to match colour of elastic

Bobbin thread to match colour of gusset

*Remember to take your time and relax – enjoy the
process of making your very own knickers!*

Cutting the pattern

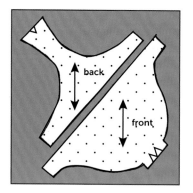

Cut out paper pattern following your size lines using the layout plan. All templates can be found at the end of this book. Make sure you use the grain lines to ensure your pattern pieces are placed on the bias. If you have pinking shears use them to cut out to stop the fabric from fraying. Cut out the gusset shape from a piece of cotton jersey using ordinary straight edge scissors.

KEY

wrong side of fabric   right side of fabric   paper pattern

APPLYING ELASTIC TIP

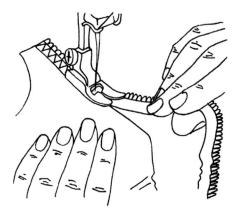

Using a scrap piece of elastic and fabric practice the following technique to apply elastic evenly. Line up the elastic to the edge of the fabric leaving any frill over the inside edge of the sewing machine foot. Set your sewing machine to zig-zag, then stitch back and forth for a couple of stitches to secure the elastic. Zig-zag stitch over the elastic, keeping it under tension by pulling a little towards yourself. Finish with a few more back stitches. Once you have perfected your technique, use the same method to apply elastic neatly and evenly to your knickers.

Making up

1. Pin together the three parts of the knickers in this order: gusset, back, then front right sides together, lining up notches. Place the pinned fabric in the sewing machine with the gusset on the underside and sew along edge with 1cm (½in) seam allowance using a straight stitch **(A)**.

2. Open out the joined together knicker and flip the gusset over into place and pin. Your raw seam edges will be concealed. Secure the gusset in place by stitching down both of the outer edges, do this on your machine, sewing 5mm (¼in) away from the edge. Trim the gusset to the exact size of your knicker to neaten if necessary **(B)**.

3. Once you have practiced and you have managed to make an even gathering of the fabric (see Applying Elastic Tip), you should start on your knickers. The elastic is placed on the right side of the fabric with any frill pointing outwards and sitting slightly over the edge of the fabric. Ensure the elastic part is on top of your knickers. Start on either the top front straight edge or top back straight edge. Continue all around the four edges, starting, finishing off and cutting the elastic at each edge. Do not elasticate the side seams.

4. Place side seams together, front to back, with right sides facing making sure you line up your elastic. Stitch across with a straight stitch, back tacking at either end **(C)**. Repeat with the other side. You should now have constructed a pair of knickers! Finish off by tying a bow with the ribbon and placing it in the centre of the front and stitching it on. Make your self a nice cup of tea!

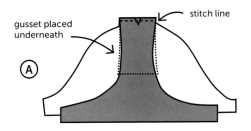

gusset placed underneath

stitch line

(A)

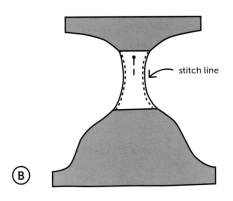

stitch line

(B)

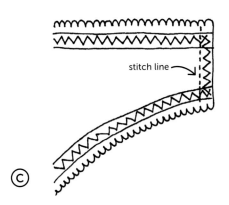

stitch line

(C)

FRENCH KNICKERS

THESE LOOSE FITTING SHORTS ARE MORE
USUALLY WORN AS NIGHTWEAR OR AS A SUMMER PYJAMA
BOTTOM. MADE FROM FINE LIBERTY TANA LAWN COTTON THEY ARE SOFT
AND FLOATY. OF COURSE, THIS STYLE OF KNICKERS WAS WORN IN THE
30S AND 40S OVER STOCKINGS AND SUSPENDER BELTS, AND THOSE WHO
COULD AFFORD IT WOULD HAVE INDULGED IN THE LUXURY OF SILK. FOR
A MODERN ALTERNATIVE WE RECOMMEND USING LIBERTY'S TANA LAWN
FABRIC FOR ITS BEAUTIFULLY SOFT TOUCH AND DRAPE.

You Will Need

1m (40in) cotton lawn fabric, at least 115cm (45in) wide

2m (2 ¼yd) lace, 1–4cm (½–1 ½in) wide depending on
the desired finish

1m (40in) elastic, 1–1.5cm (½–⅝in) wide with frilled or
crocheted edge

1m (40in) stretch lace, 2–4cm (¾–1 ½in) wide

Vintage buttons and 50cm (20in) ribbon, 5mm–2cm
(¼–¾in) wide, to decorate

Threads to match colour of elastic and fabric

*A French seam neatly covers raw edges and has the
added advantage of being stronger than a simple seam. It
is perfect for finishing off delicate fabrics such as silk
that have a tendency to fray.*

Cutting the pattern

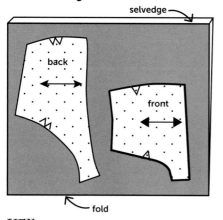

Cut out the pattern in your chosen size, using the paper pattern and following the layout plan. All templates can be found at the end of this book. Make sure you transfer all notches and markings from the pattern to your fabric.

KEY

▨ wrong side of fabric   ☐ right side of fabric   ⊡ paper pattern

Making up

1. Take a back and front and pin the wrong sides together at the side seams matching the notches. Sew together using a straight stitch and a 5mm (¼in) seam allowance **(A)**. This is the first stage in creating a French seam, which you will complete in step 2.

2. Press flat and trim the edge next to your stitch line to 3mm (⅛in). Next fold the fabric right sides together. Pin along the side seam and sew along at 5mm (¼in) to complete a French seam **(B)**. Press flat. Repeat on the other leg.

3. Lay one leg out flat with the right side up, and pin lace along the bottom edge, right sides together. Sew at 1cm (½in) from the raw edge of the fabric **(C)**.

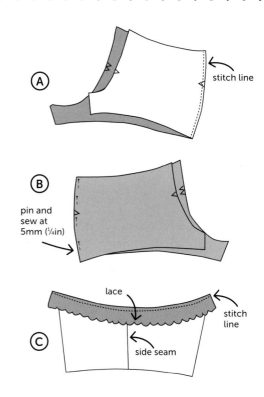

FRENCH KNICKERS

4. Lay the lace out flat, wrong side up, with the seam sitting up. Fold the seam towards the fabric, flip over so the right side is up and the seam folded under towards the fabric. Top stitch the lace in place, using colour-matched thread and a straight stitch, very close to the seam where the lace meets the fabric (D). Repeat on the second leg. The raw edge of the fabric is now covered by the lace.

5. On the first leg pin the inner leg seams wrong sides together and stitch at 5mm (¼in), then repeat the stages to create a French seam (see steps 1 and 2). Repeat (E and F) for the second leg. You will now have two legs joined with French seams.

6. Turn one leg inside out, keep the other one the right way round. Place the inside out one inside the other, lining up the inside leg seam (G).

7. Pin together the centre front and centre back seams with wrong sides together (H). Create a French seam by sewing a 5mm (¼in) seam, trimming it to 3mm (⅛in), turning right sides together and sewing a final seam (see the French seam instructions in steps 1 and 2).

8. To create the waistband start at the centre back, place stretch lace or elastic right side to right side of the fabric. Change your sewing machine setting to a small zig-zag stitch to secure the lace. Begin

with a couple of stitches forward and back. Pull the elastic slightly as you stitch to create a gather and zig-zag towards your finger (see the technique used in the Cotton Original project). Continue all the way around the top of the knickers and back tack at end to secure your stitching (I).

9. Fold the lace or elastic upwards so that the raw top edge of fabric sits behind. From the right side, flatten the knickers out and top stitch all the way around using a zig-zag (or 3-step zig-zag if you have one), to hold your waistband in place (J). The raw edge of the knickers is now concealed. Finish off your gorgeous French knickers with a ribbon bow or buttons.

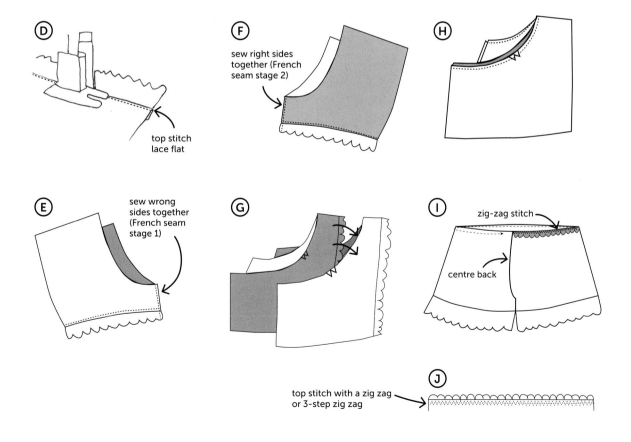

D
top stitch lace flat

F
sew right sides together (French seam stage 2)

H

E
sew wrong sides together (French seam stage 1)

G
top stitch with a zig zag or 3-step zig zag

I
zig-zag stitch
centre back

J

RIBBON TIE

THESE KNICKERS ARE NOT THE MOST PRACTICAL
THING FOR WEARING UNDER YOUR EVERYDAY CLOTHES. HOWEVER, THEY
SIT BEAUTIFULLY UNDER FULL SKIRTS OR DRESSES AND ARE A BIT OF FUN
FOR WEARING IN THE BEDROOM, AS OF COURSE THE HAND-TIED BOW CAN
BE UNDONE AS EASILY AS IT CAN BE TIED UP! WE LOVE THEM FOR THEIR
PRETTY FLIRTY FEEL ESPECIALLY WHEN MADE UP IN DELICATE FLORAL
PRINTS. WE RECOMMEND SOFT SILKY COTTON LAWN FABRIC, WHICH GIVES
YOU A SENSUOUS FEEL WHILST KEEPING THE PRACTICALITY OF WORKING
WITH COTTON. OF COURSE, IF YOU FEEL CONFIDENT YOU CAN USE SILKS OR
SATINS FOR A MORE LUXURIOUS RESULT!

You Will Need

60cm (23 ½in) cotton lawn fabric, 115cm (45in) wide
or 50cm (20in) cotton lawn fabric, 140cm (55in) wide

15 x 15cm (6 x 6in) cotton jersey for gusset

2m (2¼yd) elastic with frilled or looped edge, 1.5cm (⅝in) wide

25cm (10in) straight elastic, 5mm (¼in) wide

Button or 50cm (20in) ribbon, 1–1.5cm (½–⅝in) wide, to decorate
(optional)

Threads to match colour of elastic or lace, and fabric

Bobbin thread to match colour of gusset

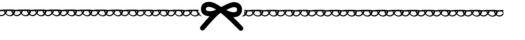

*Using a contrasting thread when sewing on the
elastic can add to the decorative affect.*

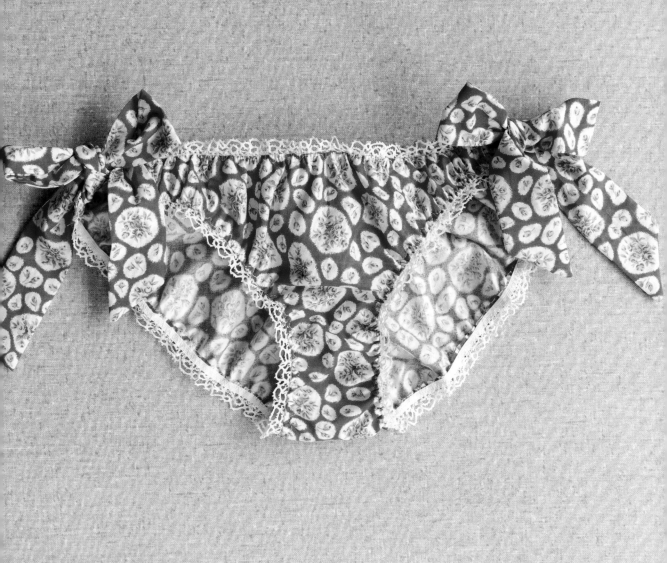

Cutting the pattern

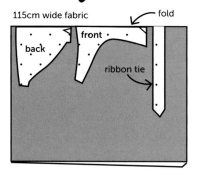

115cm wide fabric

fold

back

front

ribbon tie

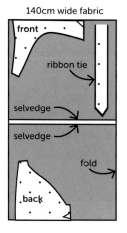

140cm wide fabric

front

ribbon tie

selvedge

selvedge

fold

back

Cut out the pattern in your chosen size, using the paper pattern and following the layout plan that matches the width of your fabric. All templates can be found at the end of this book. Make sure you transfer all notches and markings from the pattern to your fabric. Cut out a gusset shape from a piece of cotton jersey using sharp straight-edge scissors (not pinking shears).

KEY

 wrong side of fabric    right side of fabric   paper pattern

Making up

1. Pin together the three parts of the knickers in this order: gusset, back, front, with right sides together and the notches lined up. Place the pinned fabric in the machine with the gusset on the underside and sew along edge with 1cm (½in) seam allowance using a straight stitch **(A)**.

2. Open out the joined together knicker pieces and flip the gusset over into place and pin. Your raw seam edges will be concealed. Secure the gusset in place by stitching down both of the outer edges, do this on your machine sewing 5mm (¼in) from the edge. Trim the gusset to the exact size of your knickers to neaten if necessary **(B)**.

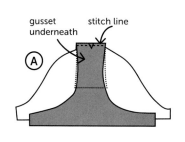

gusset underneath   stitch line

(A)

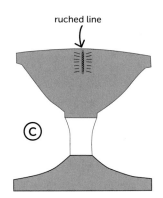

ruched line

(C)

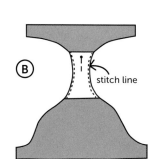

(B)

stitch line

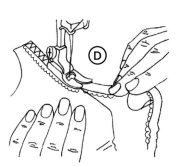

(D)

RIBBON TIE

3. To create the ruched line on the back of the knickers, take the straight piece of elastic and cut it to 6cm (2 ½in) in length. Place one end of the elastic on one of the circle markings on the wrong side of the back piece. Using a zig-zag stitch make a couple of stitches forward and backwards to secure the elastic. Leaving the needle on your sewing machine down, stretch the elastic towards you by a couple of centimetres (about an inch) and continue to sew to the other circle marking. Back tack at the end to secure, and trim the elastic to length (C).

4. Using a scrap piece of elastic practice the following technique: line up the elastic to the edge of the right side of the fabric. The straight edge of the elastic is parallel to the edge of the fabric, the frill pointing inwards. Secure with a couple of stitches. Then take the elastic and zig zag over with tension by pulling a little towards you (D). Once you have managed to make an even gathering of the fabric you should start on your knickers. Start on either the front or back straight edge (E). Continue around all four edges, starting, finishing off and cutting the elastic at each edge. Try to stitch as close to the edge as you can.

5. When you have gone round the four sides fold the elastic over so the frill is on the outside and the elastic is on the inside of the fabric. With the right side of the knickers facing you place them under the presser foot and make a couple of zig-zag stitches to secure. Then pull the knickers out flat and sew all the way around again on the outside, using a zig-zag (or a 3-step zig-zag if you have one) to hold the elastic in place. The raw edge of the fabric is now hidden by the elastic and the lacy frill is left showing over the edge (F).

6. Take one of your cut out ribbon ties and fold lengthways right sides together, pin and sew along the edge with a 5mm (¼in) seam allowance, leaving the short edge open so you can turn the ties the right way out. Trim any excess fabric if necessary and turn out. You may have to use a ruler, knitting needle or a similar device to push the end through. Press flat (G). Repeat so that you have made four ribbon ties for your knickers.

7. To attach the ribbon ties, work on the inside of the knickers and line up the end of the tie to the end of a side, laying the tie inwards towards the body of the knickers (H). Fold over the end, both ribbon tie and knickers, once (I).

Next flip back the ribbon tie to the outside. Hold it in place with your fingers (pinning doesn't really help at this stage), place it under the machine foot and sew a rectangle through all the layers with a straight stitch to secure the tie to the knickers (J). Repeat on the other three sides. Tie a bow either side and decorate with a vintage button. Mother of pearl makes a beautiful finishing touch to your one-of-a-kind knickers.

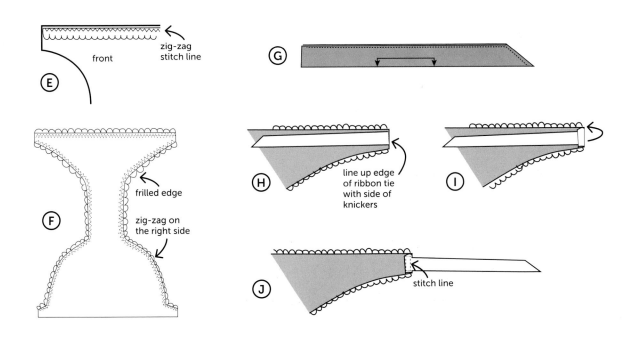

front

zig-zag stitch line

E

G

F

frilled edge

zig-zag on the right side

H

line up edge of ribbon tie with side of knickers

I

J

stitch line

RIBBON TIE

⋆ STRETCH ⋆

EVERYONE NEEDS A GOOD PAIR OF COMFY KNICKERS
AND THESE ARE THE ONES! THEY ARE A GREAT LITTLE PROJECT
FOR GETTING YOU STARTED WITH SEWING STRETCH FABRICS. YOU DON'T
NEED A SPECIALIZED MACHINE BUT YOU DO END UP WITH A PAIR OF
PANTS THAT LOOK VERY PROFESSIONAL AND 'STORE BOUGHT.' ONCE YOU
HAVE MASTERED THIS YOU'LL WANT TO MAKE MORE AND MORE. THIS IS A
GREAT PATTERN TO USE TO UP-CYCLE OLD T-SHIRTS INTO NEW KNICKERS
– ANY T-SHIRT WITH LYCRA IN IT WILL WORK. CHECK THAT THE STRETCH
IS FOUR-WAY BY STRETCHING THE FABRIC BOTH LENGTH WAYS AND
HORIZONTALLY AND MAKING SURE THERE IS ENOUGH 'PING-BACK' TO HOLD
YOUR KNICKERS UP! USING COMBINATIONS OF STRETCH LACE CAN MAKE
THESE UNDERPANTS LOOK GREAT.

You Will Need

50cm (20in) 4-way stretch fabric (we use cotton lycra
mix), only 75cm (29½in) wide

2.5m (2 ¾yd) stretch lace, 2.5–3.5cm (1–1 ⅜in) wide

50cm (20in) ribbon, 1–2cm (½–¾in) wide, to decorate

Thread to match colour of lace

*If using curved lace make sure the curves are symmetrical
on each leg. Pin one leg then mirror the curves of the lace on
the other leg, taking special care through the gusset area.*

Cutting the pattern

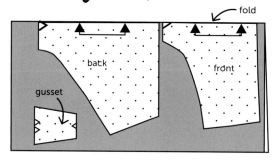

Cut out or trace off the front, back and gusset pattern pieces in your chosen size. All templates can be found at the end of this book. Fold your fabric in half, right sides together, then using the layout plan pin the pattern to the reverse of the fabric. Cut out with sharp scissors remembering to transfer all the markings and notches to your fabric.

KEY

▢ wrong side of fabric	▢ right side of fabric	▢ paper pattern

Making up

1. Lay one gusset piece right side down (this will be the lining gusset), lay the knicker back on top, right side up. Lay the other gusset piece on top right side down (this will be the outer gusset), lining up your double notches. The knicker back is sandwiched between the two gussets. Pin the three layers and sew together with a 1cm (½in) seam allowance using a straight stitch **(A)**.

2. Lay the back right side up on a table, and pull the lining gusset out flat, right side to the table under the knicker back. Leave the outer gusset right side up lying out away from the knicker back **(B)**.

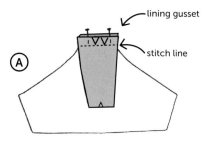

Ⓐ lining gusset / stitch line

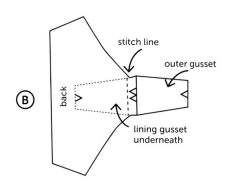

Ⓑ back / stitch line / outer gusset / lining gusset underneath

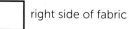

3. Place the knicker front on top of the outer gusset, right sides together, lining up the notches. Pin the pieces together (C).

4. Roll the front of the knicker over on itself towards the pin. Then roll the back of the knicker the same way, so both front and back are on top of the outer gusset piece. The gussets remain flat on the table until the next step (indicated with the dotted arrow) (D).

5. Fold the lining gusset over the top of the rolled up knickers, and line up the front notches. Pin and sew in place with a 1cm (½in) seam allowance (E).

6. This is when the magic happens! Pull the rolled up front and back through the gusset and your knickers should be in one piece with both your gusset seams hidden. Lay your knickers out flat right side up ready for applying lace edging. Lace is attached to the outside of the knickers.

7. If your lace is curved on both edges make sure the curves are symmetrical on each leg. To do this, pin one leg, then mirror the curves of the lace on the other leg taking special care through the gusset area. Pin the lace in place all the way around the knickers (F), except for the side seams. Do not stretch the lace as you pin. Change the stitch on your sewing machine to a small zig-zag, colour matching your thread to your lace. Attach your lace by sewing along the top edge carefully following the curve of the lace if necessary (G).

8. Finally line up the side seams, front to back on each side, with right sides together. Sew a 1cm (½in) seam on each side, back tacking at either end to secure. Tie a ribbon bow and sew it onto your knickers to decorate.

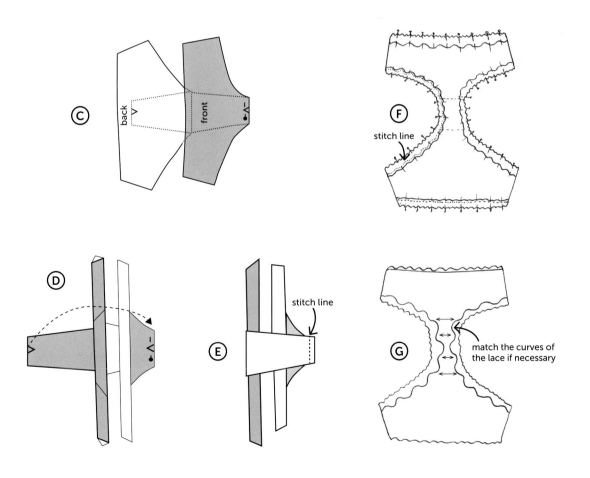

STRETCH

✶ BRAZILIAN ✶

A SLIGHTLY SAUCIER CUT ACROSS THE BOTTOM
GIVES THESE KNICKERS THEIR DISTINCTIVE SHAPE AND NAME.
THE PATTERN ALSO HAS A DIFFERENT FINISH, USING PLAIN ELASTIC AND
DECORATIVE ZIG-ZAG STITCHING TO CREATE A FRILLED EFFECT.
THE RAW EDGE OF THE FABRIC IS EDGED WITH A VERY SMALL ZIG-ZAG
OR OVERLOCK STITCH. CONTRASTING THREAD CAN ALSO BE USED TO GIVE
AN ADDITIONAL DECORATIVE EFFECT. IF YOU DO HAVE AN OVERLOCKER
(SERGER) A ROLLED HEM CAN BE USED. THE KNICKERS ARE CUT IN THREE
PIECES WITH ALL THE SEAMS CONCEALED NEATLY WITHIN THE GUSSET.
THE TECHNIQUE FOR GATHERING AND THEN NOT GATHERING IN BETWEEN
THE MARKINGS ON THE PATTERN ENSURES THE KNICKERS SIT FLAT ACROSS
THE BOTTOM. IT CAN BE MADE OUT OF ANY LIGHT WOVEN FABRIC, POPLIN,
COTTON LAWN, SILK, SATINS OR VOILES.

You Will Need

60cm (23 ½in) light woven fabric, 115cm (45in) wide

15 x 10cm (6 x 4in) cotton jersey for gusset

2m (2¼yd) white or black elastic, 5mm (¼in) wide

50cm (20in) satin ribbon, 0.5–1cm (¼–½in) wide, to
decorate

Thread to contrast with colour of fabric

*If you are lucky enough to have an overlocker (serger) you
can use this on a rolled hem setting to finish off the edges of
the knickers, alternatively a zig-zag stitch can be used.*

Cutting the pattern

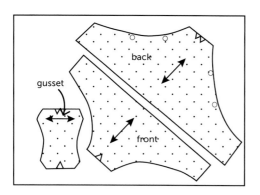

Cut out paper pattern following your size lines using the layout plan. All templates can be found at the end of this book. Back and front pieces are placed on the bias. Cut out one outer gusset from the main fabric and one gusset from cotton jersey using sharp scissors. Make sure you transfer all notches and markings from the pattern to your fabric.

KEY

 wrong side of fabric   □ right side of fabric   paper pattern

Making up

1. Lay the cotton jersey gusset on the table. Lay the knicker back on top, right side up, lining up the notches, then lay the fabric gusset on top wrong side up, lining up the notches. Pin together and sew with a straight stitch with a 1cm (½in) seam allowance **(A)**.

2. Lay the knicker back right side up on the table. Pull the jersey gusset out flat underneath the back. Leave the outer gusset right side up **(B)**.

3. Place the knicker front onto the outer gusset, lining up the front notches, with right sides together. Pin the two pieces together **(C)**.

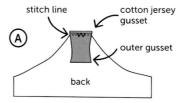

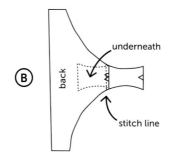

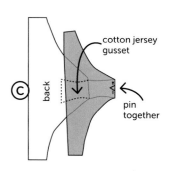

4. Roll the front of the knicker over onto itself towards the pin. Then roll the back of the knicker the same way, so both pieces sit on top of the outer gusset piece. The cotton jersey gusset remains flat at this stage **(D)**.

Fold the cotton jersey gusset over the top of the rolled up knickers and line up the front notches **(E)**. Now re-pin through all three layers of the front edge of the gusset.

Sew in place with a 1cm (½in) seam allowance, back tacking at either end **(F)**. This is the magic part: pull the rolled up front and back through the gusset and your knickers should be in one piece with both gusset seams hidden!

5. To finish off the edges of the knickers we use an overcast zig-zag stitch. The idea is that the left-hand stitch goes into the fabric and the right-hand stitch goes over the edge, binding the fabric. This creates a nice finish and looks great with a contrasting coloured thread. Zig-zag in this way around all the edges of your knickers except the side seams **(G)**. As the knicker front and back are cut on the bias the fabric will pull and naturally create a frill as you sew.

6. Sew up the side seams to create the leg holes. Place right sides together of front and back side seams on both the left and the right side. Sew together with a straight stitch and a 1cm (½in) seam allowance **(H)**.

7. Using a plain 5mm (¼in) wide elastic, measure around your hips – do not stretch the elastic – and mark with a pin. Then measure 15–20cm (6–8in) off the end and cut. Pin this evenly around the

top waistband of your knickers **(I)**. Using a zig-zag stitch with the length set short and the width set wide, sew on the inside of the knickers along the elastic, stretching it out as you sew. This will create a gather around the top of you knickers **(J)**. Contrasting threads can again look really good and add decorative detail.

8. Measure around the flat length of the leg holes and then cut elastic for each leg, two thirds the length of the measurement taken. Repeat the same method around each leg. When pinning your elastic do not stretch between the two circle markings on each side of the bottom **(J)**. This will ensure that your knickers will sit flat across your bottom and not go up your bum!

9. Make two small bows out of satin ribbon and place either side at the front to add a pretty finishing touch. Your knickers are now ready to wear.

roll

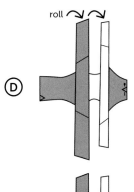

(D)

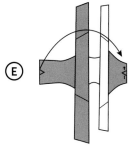

(E)

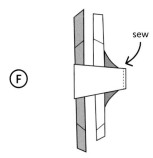

sew

(F)

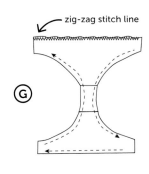

zig-zag stitch line

(G)

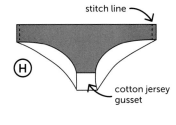

stitch line

cotton jersey gusset

(H)

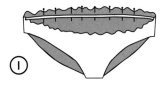

(I)

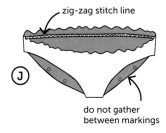

zig-zag stitch line

do not gather between markings

(J)

BRAZILIAN

VINTAGE UP-CYCLE

✦ THIS IS ONE OF OUR FAVOURITE KNICKERS TO WEAR
AND MAKE, AS EACH PAIR IS TOTALLY INDIVIDUAL AND UNIQUE.
WE LOVE THE WHOLE PROCESS FROM SOURCING THE SCARF TO ADDING
THE FINAL TOUCHES OF SILK RIBBON OR A VINTAGE BUTTON. WHEN BUYING SILK
SCARVES LOOK AT THE HEMS, A GOOD INDICATOR OF SILK IS A HAND STITCHED
ROLLED HEM. POLYESTER SCARVES TEND TO BE MACHINE STITCHED. ANOTHER
WAY OF TELLING SILK FROM MAN-MADE FABRICS IS BY BURNING A THREAD, SILK
WILL BURN WITH A FLAME, WHEREAS MAN-MADE FABRIC WILL MELT. OF COURSE
BURNING THREADS IN CHARITY SHOPS IS NOT AN OPTION, SO CHECKING THE
HEM WILL ENSURE YOU DON'T GET INTO ANY TROUBLE! THE RIBBON TIE PATTERN
NEEDS TO BE TRACED OFF AS A WHOLE PATTERN PIECE AND PLACED ON YOUR
SCARF ON THE BIAS. FOLDING SILK ACCURATELY ON THE BIAS IS TRICKY SO THIS
IS THE EASIEST WAY TO MAKE SURE YOUR PATTERN PIECE IS PLACED CORRECTLY
ON YOUR FAVOURITE PART OF YOUR SCARF. ✦

You Will Need

1 vintage silk scarf

15 x 15cm (6 x 6in) cotton jersey for gusset

2m (2 ¼yd) knicker elastic, 1.5–2.5cm (⅝–1in) wide
with a frilled or crocheted edge

2m (2 ¼yd) silk ribbon, 2–3cm (¾–1 ¼in) wide

Threads to match colour of elastic and fabric

Bobbin thread to match colour of gusset

*You can use any type of ribbon: silk, satin, grosgrain,
but we prefer silk as it keeps the knickers feeling
beautifully soft and luxurious.*

Cutting the pattern

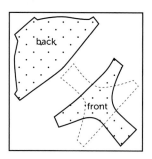

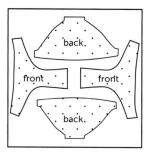

Depending on the size and pattern of your scarf you can choose to lay your pattern diagonally on the bias or on the straight grain and maybe squeeze two pairs of knickers from one scarf. Laying on the bias will mean that your knickers will have a bit more 'ease' in them. Cut out paper pattern following your size lines using your chosen layout plan. Cut out gusset shape from a piece of cotton jersey.

KEY

▦ wrong side of fabric	☐ right side of fabric	⊡ paper pattern

Your cutting out layout may need to vary from our suggestion because of the print design and size of your scarf. Often floral prints come with a border which can look great when incorporated into your design. Think of these details when laying out your pattern.

Making up

1. Pin together the three parts of the knickers in this order: gusset, back, front, with right sides together and notches lined up. Place the pinned fabric in your sewing machine with the gusset on the underside and sew along edge with 1cm (½in) seam allowance using a straight stitch **(A)**.

2. Open out the joined together knicker pieces, flip the gusset over into place and pin. Your raw seam edges will be concealed. Secure the gusset in place by stitching down both of the outer edges. Do this on your machine, sewing 5mm (¼in) away from the edge. Trim the gusset to the exact size of your knickers to neaten if necessary **(B)**.

3. Next apply the elastic using the same method as the one described in the Ribbon Tie knickers. Start in the same way on either the top front straight edge or the top back straight edge **(C)**.

4. Continue all around the four edges, starting, finishing off and cutting the elastic as you come to the end of each edge. Try to keep your stitches as close to the edge as you can. Do not elasticate the side seams.

5. When you have gone round the four sides fold the elastic over so the frill is on the outside and the

elastic is on the inside of the fabric. With the right side of the knickers facing you place them under the presser foot and do a couple of zig-zag stitches to secure. Then pull the knickers out flat and sew on the outside of your knickers all the way around again, using a zig-zag stitch (or a three-step zig-zag if you have one), to hold the elastic in place. The raw edge of the fabric is now hidden by the elastic and the lacy frill is left showing over the edge of the knickers **(D)**.

6. Now you need to attach the ribbons. Cut four pieces of ribbon 30cm (12in) long. Working on the

inside of the knickers, line up the end of the ribbon with the side edge, laying the ribbon inwards towards the body of the knickers **(E)**. Fold over the end, folding both ribbon and knicker edge, once **(F)**.

Flip the ribbon back away from the knickers. Hold it in place with your fingers (it's easier than pinning this stage) and place under the sewing machine presser foot. Sew a rectangle shape through all the layers with a straight stitch to secure the ribbon to the knickers **(G)**. Repeat on the other three sides. Tie a bow and if you have a vintage button this is the time to add it for a finishing touch.

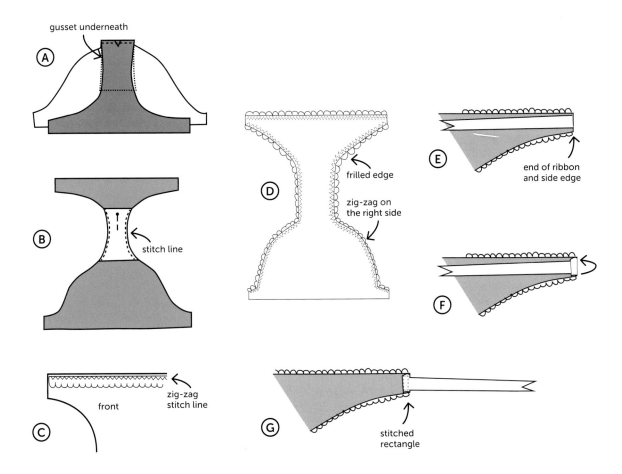

Templates
FOR
KNICKERS

ALL TEMPLATES MUST BE ENLARGED BY 200%

FULL SIZED TEMPLATES CAN BE DOWNLOADED
FROM THE STITCH CRAFT CREATE WEBSITE AT:

http://ideas.sewandso.co.uk/patterns/

UK DRESS SIZES ARE MARKED ON THE TEMPLATES – SEE BELOW
FOR A FULL CONVERSION CHART TO US DRESS SIZES

UK	6	8	10	12	14	16	18	20	22
US	2	4	6	8	10	12	14	16	18

COTTON ORIGINAL

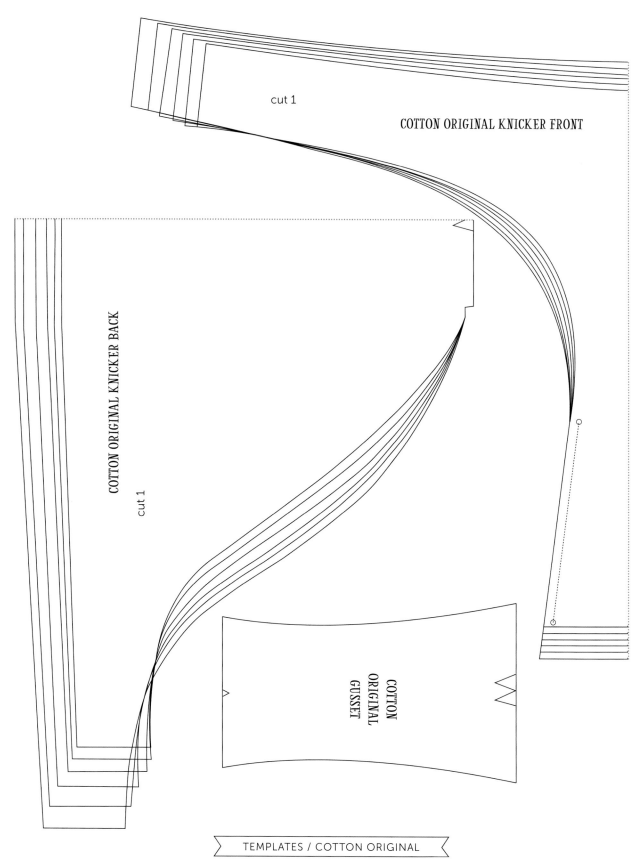

cut 1

COTTON ORIGINAL KNICKER FRONT

COTTON ORIGINAL KNICKER BACK

cut 1

COTTON ORIGINAL GUSSET

COTTON ORIGINAL KNICKER FRONT

grain line

8 10 12 14 16 18

COTTON ORIGINAL KNICKER BACK

grain line

8 10 12 14 16 18

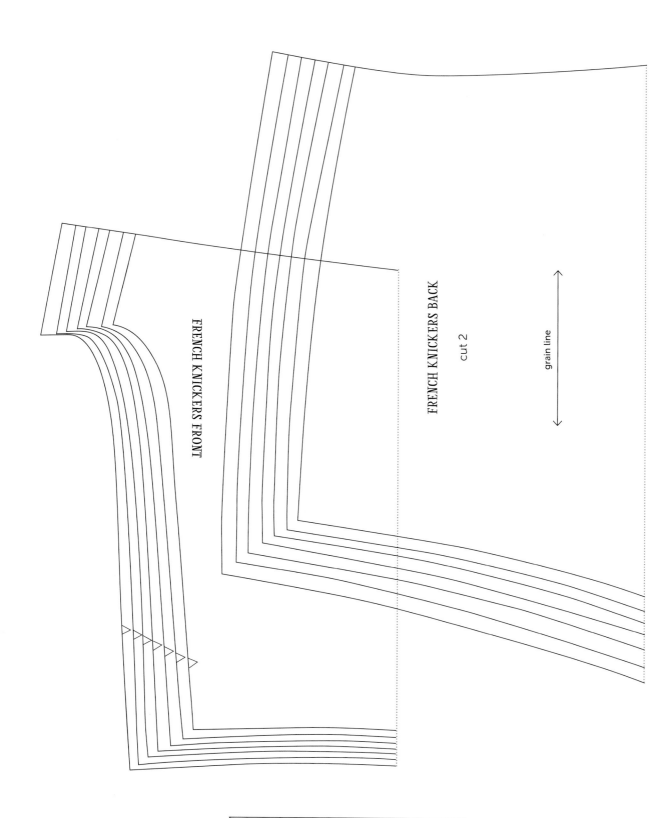

FRENCH KNICKERS FRONT

FRENCH KNICKERS BACK

cut 2

grain line

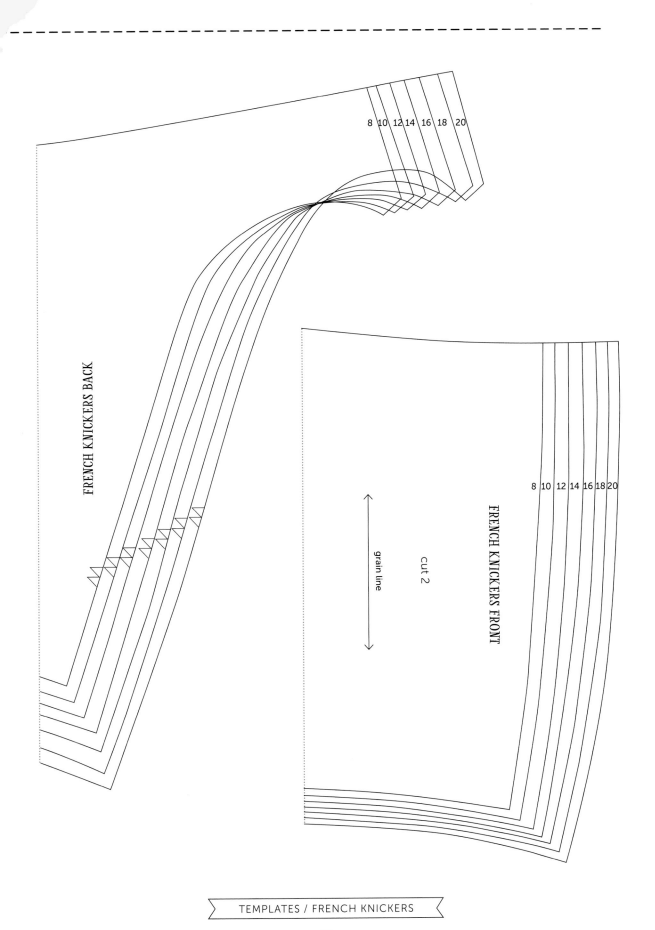

FRENCH KNICKERS BACK

FRENCH KNICKERS FRONT

8 10 12 14 16 18 20

8 10 12 14 16 18 20

grain line

cut 2

RIBBON-TIE

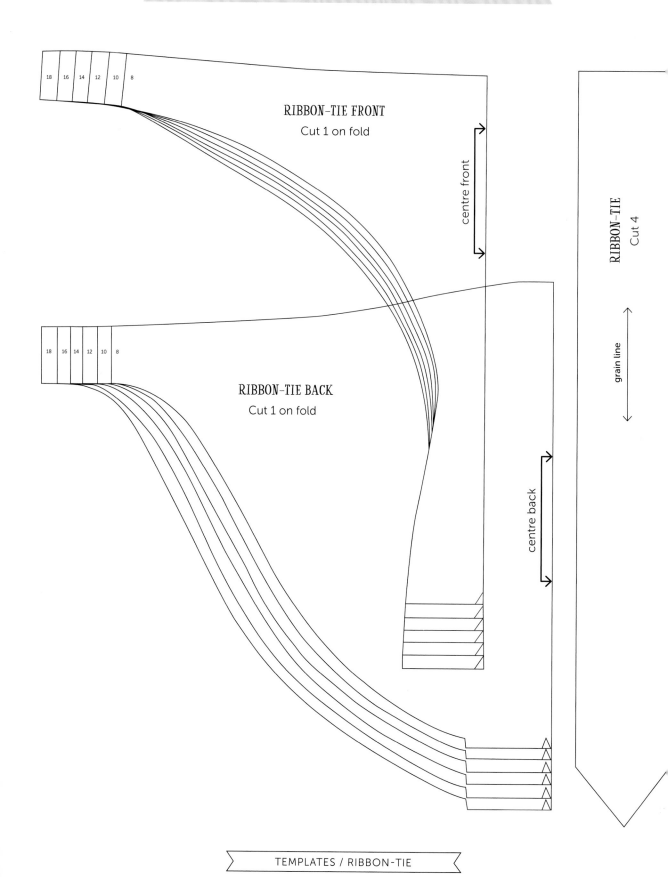

RIBBON-TIE FRONT
Cut 1 on fold

centre front

18 16 14 12 10 8

RIBBON-TIE BACK
Cut 1 on fold

18 16 14 12 10 8

centre back

RIBBON-TIE
Cut 4

grain line

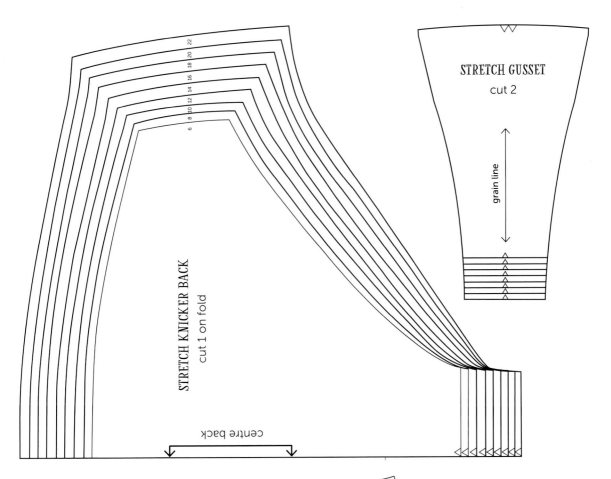

STRETCH GUSSET
cut 2

grain line

STRETCH KNICKER BACK
cut 1 on fold

centre back

22 20 18 16 14 12 10 8 6

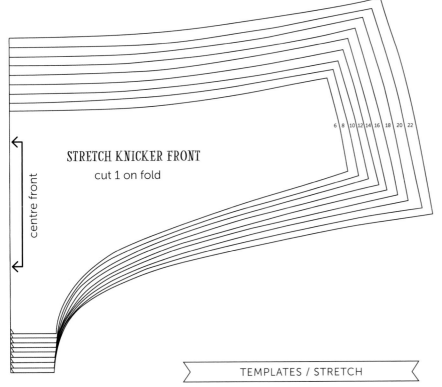

STRETCH KNICKER FRONT

cut 1 on fold

centre front

6 8 10 12 14 16 18 20 22

BRAZILIAN

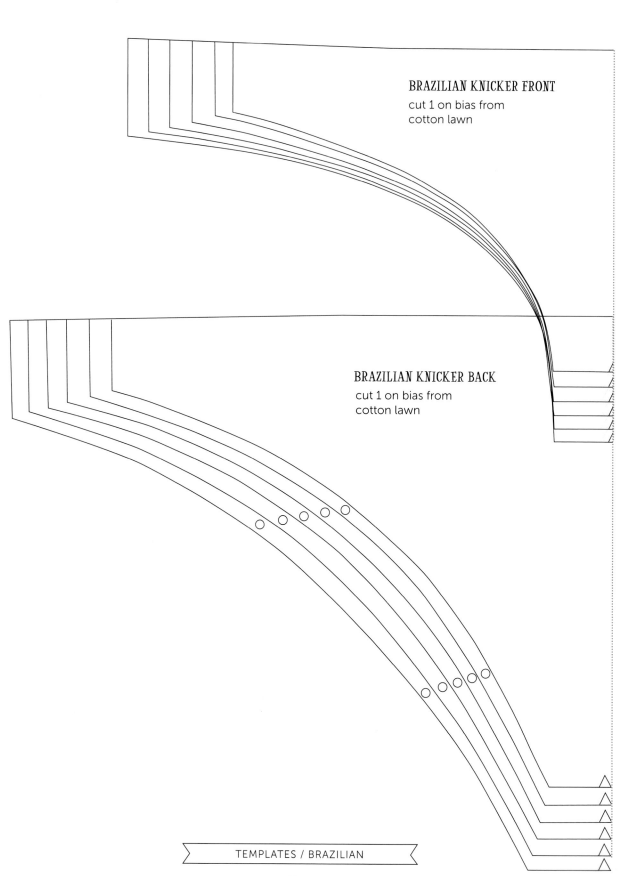

BRAZILIAN KNICKER FRONT
cut 1 on bias from
cotton lawn

BRAZILIAN KNICKER BACK
cut 1 on bias from
cotton lawn

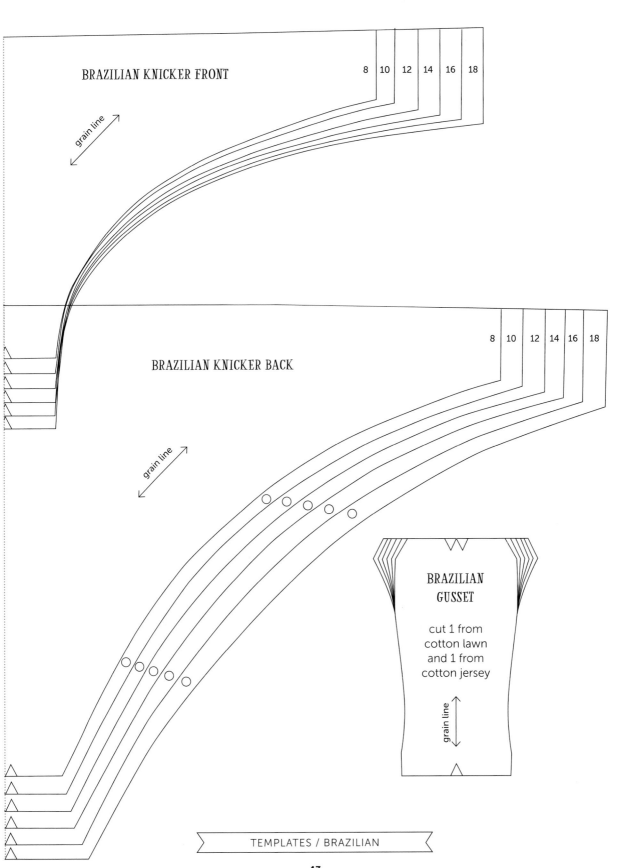

BRAZILIAN KNICKER FRONT

| 8 | 10 | 12 | 14 | 16 | 18 |

grain line

BRAZILIAN KNICKER BACK

| 8 | 10 | 12 | 14 | 16 | 18 |

grain line

BRAZILIAN
GUSSET

cut 1 from
cotton lawn
and 1 from
cotton jersey

grain line

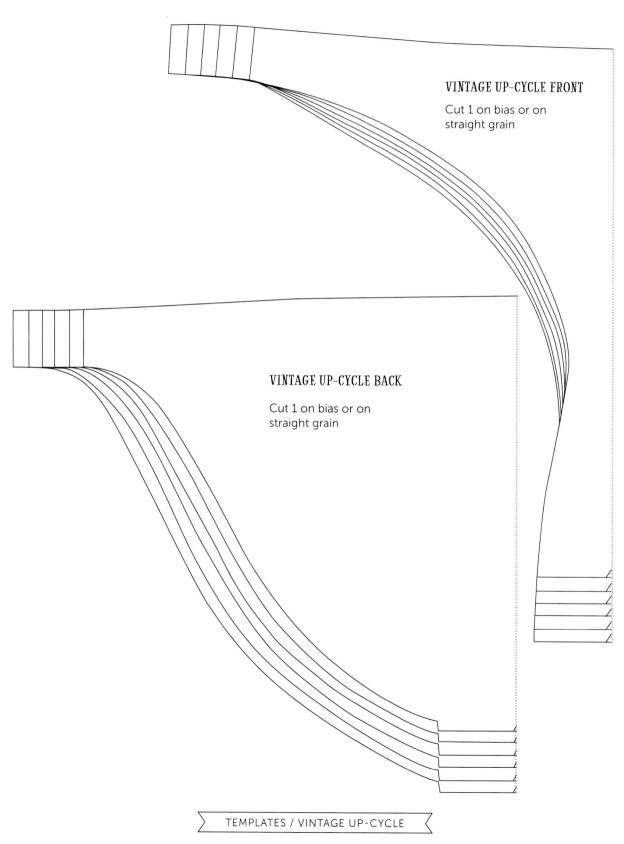

VINTAGE UP-CYCLE FRONT

Cut 1 on bias or on
straight grain

VINTAGE UP-CYCLE BACK

Cut 1 on bias or on
straight grain

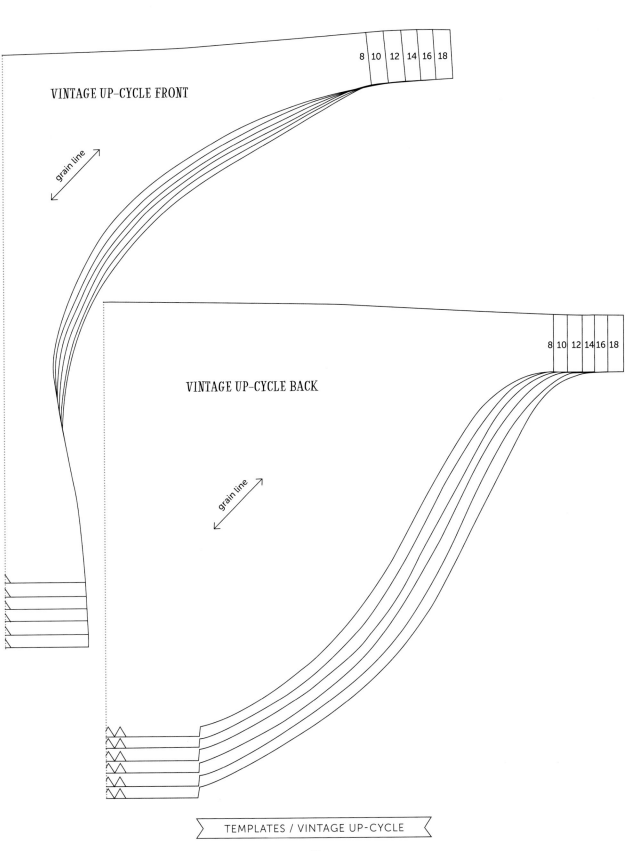

VINTAGE UP-CYCLE FRONT

grain line

8 | 10 | 12 | 14 | 16 | 18

VINTAGE UP-CYCLE BACK

grain line

8 | 10 | 12 | 14 | 16 | 18

TEMPLATES / VINTAGE UP-CYCLE

About Us

Delia and Erika met while studying garment construction and pattern cutting in 2002. By 2004 they had started to make their own range of children's wear which they named Flo-Jo after their children, Florence and Jonah who were the best of friends and perfect models! They then began to make 50s style dresses and the knickers to match. They went on to make silky ribbon tie knickers and super frilly burlesque styles.

The Flo-Jo stall was a regular at fairs and festivals. In 2010 they made the original knicker making kit and as sales grew they started to sell the kits wholesale. They soon outgrew their small studio and opened their shop on the famous independent high street called Gloucester Road in Bristol.

Their colourful fabric and haberdashery store is also a vibrant creative workshop space where they run sewing classes and parties. Flo-Jo has a range of other sewing kits which is growing all the time.

www.flojoboutique.co.uk

Our thanks to ...

Rose May, Finn Kay, Diana Child, José Peto and Florence, Jonah and Django for all their support and inspiration.

Suppliers

KNICKER ELASTICS, STRETCH LACES AND STRETCH JERSEY

www.flojoboutique.co.uk

LIBERTY TANA LAWN COTTONS

www.liberty.co.uk/Online

www.flojoboutique.co.uk

STRETCH JERSEY

www.artgalleryfabrics.co.uk

www.flojoboutique.co.uk

SEWING SUPPLIERS

www.sewandso.co.uk

END.

A DAVID & CHARLES BOOK

© F&W Media International, Ltd 2016

David & Charles is an imprint of F&W Media International, Ltd
Pynes Hill Court, Pynes Hill, Exeter, EX2 5AZ
F&W Media International, Ltd is a subsidiary of F+W Media, Inc
10151 Carver Road, Suite #200, Blue Ash, OH 45242, USA

Text and Designs © Delia Adey & Erika Peto
Layout and Photography © F&W Media International, Ltd 2016

First published in the UK and USA in 2016

Delia Adey & Erika Peto have asserted their right to be identified as authors of
this work in accordance with the Copyright, Designs and Patents Act, 1988.

A catalogue record for this book is available from the British Library.

ISBN-13: 978-1-4463-0633-8 paperback
ISBN-10: 1-4463-0633-X paperback
ISBN-13: 978-1-4463-7463-4 PDF
ISBN-10: 1-4463-7463-7 PDF
ISBN-13: 978-1-4463-7464-1 EPUB
ISBN-10: 1-4463-7464-5 EPUB

10 9 8 7 6 5 4 3 2 1

Acquisitions Editor: Sarah Callard

Desk Editor: Michelle Patten

Project Editor: Jane Trollope

Art Editor: Anna Wade

Photographer: Jason Jenkins

Production Manager: Beverley Richardson

F+W Media publishes high quality books on a wide range of subjects.

For more great book ideas visit: www.sewandso.co.uk

Layout of the digital edition of this book may vary depending on reader
hardware and display settings.